THE PARENTING 5

The Parenting 5: Sensory Motor Play for Little People

Toddler Education Services Pty Ltd
ourdomesticmontessori@gmail.com

Copyright © Ruth Barker 2014
The moral right of the author has been asserted.
All rights reserved.
Without limiting the rights under copyright reserved above,
no part of the publication may be reproduced, stored in or transmitted,
in any form or by means (electronic, mechanical, photocopying,
recording or otherwise), without the prior written permission of both
the copyright owner and the publisher of this book.

Text/cover design Georgina Collis, Inspiration Please
Images from Toddler Education Services Pty Ltd / Montessori 1:1
Montessori Child
From Little Things
Cleverstuff

Edition: 1st ISBN Print 978-0-9923103-0-1

ISBN E book: 978-0-9923103-1-8

National Library of Australia

*These books are dedicated to all
the beautiful children that I have worked with
in the past 28 years. You have taught me all
that there is to be found in life.*

*In memory of my own mother
Olive Florence Sally Barker, who nurtured
me for the first ten years of my life.*

*Also, dedicated to my father Jack Barker,
his wife and my stepmother Eileen and my Uncle
Tom Barker. Growing up on our property meant
I had the best sensory motor experience a
child could ever want. I thank them for
this early opportunity.*

*And with love to my husband, Kevin Grover,
who encourages me to share all that I am.*

CONTENTS

About the Author i

Foreword v

Safety Note ix

Introduction 1

1. Preparing the Environment 7

2. Work Endeavours 11

3. Practicing Skills and Functional Play 21

4. Practicing Skills 25

5. Functional Play 39

6. Ten Recipes for Sensory Motor Fun 55

References and Recommendations 63

ABOUT THE AUTHOR

Ruth Barker was raised on a remote wheat and sheep property in Western Australia. She knew she would work with children from a very early age, as she would 'teach' her toys in the shearing shed.

Ruth went to Swanleigh Boarding Hostel in Perth where she was a Sunday school teacher, before going on to Edith Cowan University to study a Degree in Social Science, majoring in Child Development and Family Studies with a minor study in Applied Science (Consumer).

She spent a number of years working with children in the United Kingdom where she fell in love with the ideas of Dr. Maria Montessori. Ruth returned to Australia to study a Diploma of Montessori Education (Preschool).

From 2001 to 2011 Ruth was the Directress of a small preschool program in Adelaide, South Australia. Then in 2012 it closed and Ruth began Montessori 1:1, a successful business working with toddlers and young children making the transition to school. She specialised in the one to one mode of engaging children and showing parents and carers how to prepare early childhood environments.

In 2013 Ruth commenced Toddler Education Services Pty Ltd as an Education Consultant. She wrote the first of The Parenting 5 series and began speaking with groups of parents and carers about preschool development and the Montessori method.

In 2014 Montessori 1:1 and Toddler Education Services Pty Ltd merged together. Ruth consults in the home, presents seminars and writes as a columnist for websites and magazines. She educates little people in her private practice where her passions include early literacy development, helping children with special needs and writing children's books.

The first book in the Parenting 5 series, Practical and Independent Little People was showcased at The Montessori Australia Early Childhood Education and Care Conference on the Gold Coast in March 2014, to a pleasing reception. It is available in both print and e book and acts as the precursor for this book and the remaining to come.

Ruth's work can be accessed at:
www.toddlereducationservices.com.au

This website includes links to her books, articles and blog, recently described by one American University in the top 100 for education.

Find Ruth on Instagram or Facebook:
www.instagram.com/ruthbarker1970
www.facebook.com/Montessori11

Ruth has worked with hundreds of children in many applications over the past twenty-eight years.

Here are some of the recent testimonial statements:

"Fantastic book, so easy to read and understand! Thank you! I cannot wait for Book Two and really looking forward to meeting you soon Ruth!"
Cherie.

"I am just writing to say a HUGE thank you to you! I cannot believe the turn around in our home in the past week. I have been implementing the techniques we have spoken about and that are contained in your book and I am truly amazed at the changes I have seen in J. He is so much happier and I feel like I am finally doing something right! I took him out and about today to do some jobs (the sort of thing that I usually avoid at all cost) and he was an absolute angel! We had such a great time that I'm a bit sad that he has (childcare) tomorrow!
I have been truly blessed to have the opportunity to meet you and cannot thank you enough for the care and

patience you have shown with J. I look forward to continuing to work with you as I know that I certainly have a long way to go but I at least know that I have found the right path."
Bianca.

"I'm currently reading your book and calculating how many copies I'd need to ensure that I can give one to every new parent who starts in our 'Nido' Montessori Playgroup at Jescott! We definitely have some collaborating to do Ruth Barker!"
Jessica, Head of Jescott Montessori School and Montessori Child Shop, Adelaide, Australia.

FOREWORD

Welcome to The Parenting 5. Over many years parents and carers have asked for practical guidance in the home or childcare setting, preferably without the jargon that comes with early childhood philosophies and behaviour management theories. The Parenting 5 comprises of five books to support parents and carers in developing environments that will assist preschool children to reach potential. Each book offers the application of advice through simple words and photography.

The books consist of:

1. Practical and Independent Little People

2. Sensory Motor Play for Little People

3. Developing Language and Literacy

4. Developing the Mathematical Mind

5. The World Around Them

The Parenting 5 series is best read in chronological order.

Experience throughout the early years lays the foundation for both neurological and physical wellbeing. An excellent early environment delivers readiness for life. Never again is there a period that is so influential on the make up of the human being.

"The first 6 yrs of life are when the majority of our brain architecture is formed. The exceptionally strong influence early experience on brain architecture makes the early years of life a period of great opportunity and great vulnerability. Critical aspects of brain architecture begin to be shaped before and after birth and many fundamental aspects of architecture are established well before a child enters school."
Centre on the Developing Child at Harvard University.

"Children come into the world with unlimited potential for delight and immediately commence the awe inspiring task of self-construction. The prime matter for this great work they find in their environment."
Renilde Montessori, The Common Sense of Montessori Pedagogy.

Young children have innate traits that allow development to occur without much influence from the parent or carer. Children draw information incessantly from their environment to build neural pathways through a need to be independent, to show attention and concentration, a desire for self motivated exploration and to be creative, amongst other tendencies. All the adult need do is provide a prepared environment that allows this natural process to manifest.

Preschoolers require pursuits they can actively engage with their hands. The Parenting 5 books emphasise life skills and sensory and motor (movement) activities as the most important modes for early development.

Time spent in front of television or computers should be limited as there are better ways to build good brains and strong bodies!

Towards three and a half to four years there is a neurological shift towards abstraction and the ability to understand symbolism. Should the children show an interest, this is the time to begin numeracy and phonetics. A small component of screen time may be introduced, if so desired, as long as it is realistic and supports learning.

Human relationships are also important to children's development. These important connections are based on a culture of common beliefs, values and clearly defined limits for behaviour, which are effectively demonstrated by all members of the family or group.

Please also note a strong emphasis on economics and promoting a sustainable environment throughout the books. The focus is on providing an environment on a budget and by using common household items rather than relying on many expensive commercial toys to initiate activity.

You will find beautiful images of materials pertinent to Sensory and Motor Activity in this book. Many of these images come from:

- Toddler Education Services Pty Ltd / Montessori 1:1 (Ruth's own program for children)
- Montessori Child
- From Little Things
- Cleverstuff

Links to these stores are available at the rear.

Enjoy!

SAFETY NOTE

Every endeavour should be taken for children to be provided with a safe and healthy environment. Parents and carers are encouraged to supervise at all times.

Ruth Barker takes no responsibility for any unsafe practices as a result of the use of these books.

The books include the use of small parts as an aid to learning. A safe and healthy environment occurs when children are constantly watched and cared for.

INTRODUCTION

"Children show an innate desire for movement as this is the key to a strong foundation. Children explore the world through the senses and absorb stimuli in the given environment" (source unknown).

Sensory Motor Play for Little People is a guide for parents and carers of young children from two through six years of age. It introduces sensory and motor activity associated with the endeavour of work and functional play, as necessary to healthy human development.

Gone are the days that it is believed children start learning when they go to formal school. Current research and brain scanning indicates that the neurons of the brain develop up to eighty percent of their foundation pathways by six years of age.

This makes the first years of life incredibly important!

Supported by an environment of good nutrition, loving care and sensory and motor activity, learning begins from birth! All baby mammals require these essentials to physically and mentally grow. Motivation comes from both innate traits (nature) and lessons demonstrated by parent animals that also give their babies a lot of time to play (nurture).

The needs of human babies are no different!

Through sensory and motor activity in a prepared environment little humans thrive in two major ways:

1. By absorbing information through the senses of vision, touch, hearing, smell and taste, children tune into their environment and make sense of what is in the world around them.

2. By manipulating objects with fine motor skills (the small muscles of the hand) and engaging their gross muscles through action, this assists in increasing strength, stamina and coordination particularly of the core, limbs and hands.

Children should move freely as much as possible. Natural posture and movement should not be restricted by modern parenting aids, such as those that force children to sit in unnatural positions before they are biologically ready. These are simple assistors to parents but unfortunately they don't provide what's best for children.

Engaging in sensory and motor activity causes the nerves of the human body to transmit impulses along the nerve pathways that connect the senses and the muscles to the brain. This in turn builds neurons and lays the foundation of the mind. Along with an innate ability to self-explore and absorb information from the prepared environment little humans become in charge of their own development.

There is some natural physiological pruning that is done by the brain after this intense period of neural growth. This results in the foundation of the brain being set. The intensity of this pattern of growth and trimming is not repeated during any other period of human life.

Remember this?

"Give me the child when he is seven and I will give you the man" (Seven Up Series, 1964).

It's not a fallacy at all!

When sensory and motor activity is conducted effectively, children also develop a solid neurological foundation for:

- Attention and concentration that is considered by some

psychologists as the most important mode of success for the future of children's academic life.

• The development of the eye, that includes visual discrimination - the ability to find something within a group of similar things, as well as training the eye with tracking in preparation for reading.

• Acquiring language skills such as a vast vocabulary and reciprocal communication.

• Information processing and problem solving that is termed as the development of cognition.

• Pre-mathematical skills like the emergence of one to one correspondence (a single item is 'one', with another it is 'two'), object sorting and measuring quantity.

• Social skills and respect for others.

• An understanding of ones own emotions brought about through environmental experience.

• Success with literacy and mathematics, as sensory and motor activity provides many of the pre-requisite skills for academics.

When there is a fault in the neural pathways (commonly termed as a Sensory Processing Disorder), learning can be somewhat challenged and adult intervention may be necessary to enhance the pathways leading to the brain. This may include children who are not as physically strong or coordinated, have decreased language and communication skills, may be more limited with social and emotional maturation and less ready to pursue academia. Intervention that occurs as early as possible is a terrific support for children who require the enhancement of the neural pathways for future success.

The remainder of this book demonstrates how to set up the environment, defines work endeavours and functional play and provides ample examples of both.

"It's a guide to activity for young children, all here in one place, captured in simple words and pictures. This has been a dream many years in the making. Helping parents and children is what I do" (Barker, 2014).

Chapter 1
PREPARING THE ENVIRONMENT

In book one Practical and Independent Little People, the preparation of the environment was discussed as essential to promoting independence and to becoming a practical human being. With the addition of both sensory and motor activity, potential is further boosted.

Children thrive through sensory and motor activity derived from work endeavours or functional play in the home and/or childcare environments.

These environments do not need to be overwhelming places of chaos with excessive stimulation and noise. They ought to be a place where nature can unfold, where children can explore motives and absorb information freely and where they can thrive in peace at their own pace.

Of course, it is immensely important that the activities meet the developmental level of the children and that it coincides with the windows of opportunity for learning.

The windows of opportunity are commonly found in Montessori texts.

Here is a simple list taken from How to Raise an Amazing Child (Seldin, 2007).

Order - Order and routine are imperative for children from two years of age until late preschool.

Sensory Exploration - Begins from birth but from two years of age, through to late preschool, it is most apparent.

Movement - Intensely sensitive in the first year of life and continues through until late preschool.

Language - Language acquisition is important to children from birth to six years of age.

Academic Subjects - Writing is the first area of academics to naturally come and always precedes reading. These literary pursuits can begin anywhere from three to five years of age. Adults should wait for these natural phenomena to occur, rather than pressuring children into something they are not ready to do. Mathematics comes later, towards the end of preschool.

"Loosely, before the age of three years children are open to moving freely and learning through sensory exploration in a suitably prepared environment and post this stage, application can be given to what has been previously absorbed from the environment by increasing abstraction and academia" (Barker, 2014).

There is no point giving the early preschooler stimuli that is beyond their years. This is because successes through exploration lead to confidence, which in turn build self-esteem and a healthy self-concept. Presenting experiences that children are not prepared for will most likely result in a sense of failure.

Below is a list of the other requirements in the environment for children:

1. Little children manage better when they are provided an ongoing, yet flexible routine so they are aware of what comes next, what they need and what they need to do.

2. Children should be provided with furniture and tools that are their size so they can manage for themselves.

3. Prepare the environment with these furnishings and tools in every space that they work and play. This includes the play area, the kitchen and laundry, the bedroom, the bathroom and toilet and outdoors.

4. Limit the number of items in each space by displaying things beautifully to encourage children to put them away after use.

5. Ask yourself if what is prepared allows the children to follow through the whole process. Does it contain all the items they require?

6. Connect with children at eye level, use clear articulate language and show them the simple steps needed to accomplish the activity.

7. Have behavioural limits and expectations that are known from the start. How will children manage each step from the beginning through to putting away the materials used?

8. Allow children time to explore and enjoy the activity for themselves without interruption, unless they are misusing it.

9. Remain calm when a mistake, spill or breakage occurs because children are simply developing and learning.

10. In time repeat a step or increase learning to the next stage of the activity, dependent on readiness and accomplishment.

11. When children want to assist in everyday life, try to allow it, for this teaches them to self-manage in readiness for life.

Chapter 2

WORK ENDEAVOURS

In Practical and Independent Little People (Barker, 2013) the idea of life skills was discussed as a way to promote practicality and independence in children. In this second book these life skills will be termed work endeavours and are reviewed for their pertinence to brain development from a sensory and motor activity perspective.

When little children have access to well designed spaces and are able to use the tools needed for work in each area of the home or childcare environment, they absorb information through their muscles and senses, along the neural pathways to the brain itself. This causes the further neuron development in the brain.

Not only does work promote practicality and independence, it makes the physical body stronger and stimulates brain growth, develops discipline and good life habits such as focus and persistence.

Work endeavours are also the skills children need to manage in everyday life. The specifics of these skills reflect their own personal culture. This makes the work beneficial for physical and neurological development but essential to understand what happens in their future, as they grow toward adulthood.

Who will show them, for example, how to prepare and clean their environment, how to grow and make food and be sustainable in their practice?

The need for learning work skills has become particularly apparent in modern society due to the need to work, a lack of 'time' and the use of an abundance of electronic gadgets. These conditions do not support the nature or needs of children and may lead to the children being unable to function effectively and happily in their adult lives.

In book one work endeavours were apparent in the following spaces in the home:

- The play and learning area
- The kitchen and laundry
- The bedroom, bathroom and toilet
- The garden environment

This book will now embellish on the types of work endeavour and the tools available for each of these spaces. It is not suggested that children should undertake all of these tasks, nor should adults expect to purchase everything in this book.

1. The play and learning area:

"Provide a cleaning centre so that the children can sweep (and mop) the floors, dust, spray, wipe (and scrub) tables and chairs, (wash windows), manage spills and breakages (safety first)... water plants and design with flowers" (Barker, 2013).

Of course what is essential with cleaning processes, is that the work is developmentally appropriate for the children using the space. It is important to build these skills up as time goes by.

The following tools are conducive to this space:

• A broom with dustpan and brush.

• A bucket, a mop, a scrubbing brush, a window cleaner, a spray bottle and cloths for cleaning.

• Children must have access to water and mild detergents. These can be found at a sink by using a step. There are many wonderful steps available from Montessori suppliers that are safety wise.

www.montessorichild.com.au/products/little-helper-kitchen-stand

• A misting container for misting plants and a selection of vases for flower arranging.

• The shelving in the play and learning area of the home are best organized with trays and baskets to assist order.

2. The kitchen and laundry:

"In the kitchen provide all the tools applicable to the stage of development... include tools for cooking with adults, food preparation, crockery and cutlery for laying out their space... young children can set and clear the

table, wash dishes and load and unload the dishwasher... children can sort clothes from the washing machine, they can peg clothes and cloths to a small line (and fold clothes and cloths) and they can take care of their pets" **(Barker, 2013).**

Again, it is important to think about the type of activity that is pertinent to the individual based on their skill level. Continue to develop the skills in small steps in the kitchen and laundry area.

Use some of the following tools to help children to complete their work endeavours:

• A cooking outfit to use in the kitchen.

• Some child-sized cooking equipment and utensils for

children to use that aren't overwhelmingly large. These include a selection of bowls, jugs and tools regularly used, such as a sifter.

• Children require tools, such as a scrubbing brush for cleaning food before cooking, as well as one for washing up afterwards.

• Use a selection of choppers or knives for cutting, knives for spreading, tongs and spoons for transferring food.

• Other food preparation ideas may include; mashing, grating food, making juice, using a mortar and pestle and using a grinder (supervision is suggested when using coffee beans).

• Other endeavours may include using a garlic press, a blender, a bread machine or a pasta machine.

• Children may use crockery and cutlery to assist in setting the table which is wonderful for the connection between the members of the family or group.

• In the laundry a low fold out line and either wooden dolly pegs or household pegs are useful for children.

3. The bedroom, the bathroom and the toilet:

In the bedroom, bathroom and toilet, children need their child–sized tools of self-care presented to them with order. These items, such as hair and hand brushes, teeth cleaning needs, bathing sponges, buckets and baskets for clean, wet or dirty clothes are best presented with only the components that are required to complete a task. This information is available in Practical and Independent Little People.

4. The garden environment:

"Children enjoy planting seeds, weeding, sweeping, raking, and watering… (they may also look after their pets, work with real tools, recycling and taking out rubbish)" (Barker, 2013).

There is now a wonderful array of child-sized tools to be used in the outdoor environment to encourage children to work in the garden.

Chapter 3
PRACTICING SKILLS AND FUNCTIONAL PLAY

A prepared environment should be rich with activities to practice meaningful skills and engage functional play, otherwise it is common for children to be in chaos, bored for extended periods, or to be attached to electronic gadgets or television.

There are often too many underutilized toys that offer little to children's development, break budgets through overt commercialism, destroy the environment and act as emotional connectors when parents are otherwise engaged.

What if the children pursued activity that helped them in real life, where development was truly taking place?

What if peace and harmony resided in the home and childcare setting instead of chaos, boredom or reliance on gadgets and television?

What if the equipment wasn't that expensive and didn't fill the environment with garbage?

What if children were truly in touch with their world and

the adults in it, instead of disassociated?

What if an adult took the time to prepare the environment in each space so that the children had access to everything they require to practice skills and play with function?

And, what if adults were actually adding value to children's lives?

It can happen, with a little organization and a few simple lessons!

Why?

- To open up sensory awareness of the world around the children

- To build fine motor development and gross body physicality

- To enhance the neural pathways and the growth of the brain

- To build attention and concentration skills

- To build life skills of focus, persistence and sticking to a task

- To give children the skills they need to manage life in the future

- To enhance pre-academic development through developing grips, visual discrimination, one to one correspondence, pre-mathematics skills and so on

- To develop a sense of accomplishment resulting in confidence

- To be leaders and not followers, in their community

What if:

"The adult took book one and prepared the environment for the children and then set out the equipment which already exists and that of purchase, to give lessons in life and functional play.

Show them!

Observe them!

Further their skills!

Then watch them normalize; watch them become in tune

with their world, watch the chaos go, watch the boredom go, put the electronic gadgets away and turn the television off for a while. Inspire the children and prepare them for life" (Barker, 2014).

The following two chapters of this book are a dictionary of activities to help in skill practice and play that is functional to development.

Chapter 4

PRACTICING SKILLS

When preparing the environment for the practice of skills, it is important to remember that the work must be realistic and engage a whole cycle of activity to promote independence.

"Wherever possible please try to engage the child - whether in the home or in the classroom - in real, purposeful work that follows a complete cycle... the isolated experiences need to be utilized in broader contexts that are relevant to the child's daily routines... don't just present a spooning tray (for instance); ensure the child is

able to also use a measuring spoon in a recipe… don't just offer a sponging exercise; ensure that the child has access to sponges and the opportunity to actually clean up spills… ideally, experience should be real, purposeful and should follow a complete cycle of setting-up, activity and packing-up" (Langford, 2014).

The following questions are important to consider when setting up:

1. What is it you want to show your children to add into their skill set?

2. What is the purpose of the activity? Is it useful to real life and how will it add to life in the future?

3. Do you have all that is needed to complete the entire cycle from set up to practice and then, cleaning up?

4. Are the tools placed where the children can reach them, in a spot that follows the adage "a place for everything and everything in its place"?

5. Is the equipment child-sized and in good order?

6. Have you shown the children where to find everything and where to put it away?

7. Do the children have trays or baskets to set up their practice skills?

8. Have you shown its use in simple steps, building up the skills as time goes by?

9. Are you an adult who interrupts children when they are managing fine or when they wish to repeat a skill? And if so, what can you do to correct this behaviour?

Here is a list of the tools to use for practicing skills:

• Ceramic or glass jugs, pots, a teapot, cups and funnels for pouring liquid, rice or grain. Prepare these on a tray and add a small sponge or hand brush for spills.

• Use tongs or tweezers for transferring such things as real or fake food, pompoms and cotton wool, between jars, pots or dishes. Ice cube trays are of use here too. Colour and type sorting activities can also be given.

- Either work with a baster, a pipette, a syringe or an eyedropper for mixing water with or without colour. Set this out on a tray that contains a funnel and a sponge for drying spills.

- Spoons, which may include teaspoons, dessertspoons, measuring spoons, a ladle or a balling spoon, for transferring food or liquid between ceramic or glass containers on a tray.

- A set of measuring jugs or cups and measuring spoons to use with food such as pasta, flour, bread mix or water. A set of kitchen scales compliments this practice.

- Implements such as a wooden spoon, a rotary mixer or a spatula, used for mixing.

• Choppers, a variety of knives or a pizza wheel for cutting and a knife for spreading. Teach children to set these out on a tray, chopping board or plate.

• A vegetable peeler, hand held or mechanical for peeling vegetables and fruit.

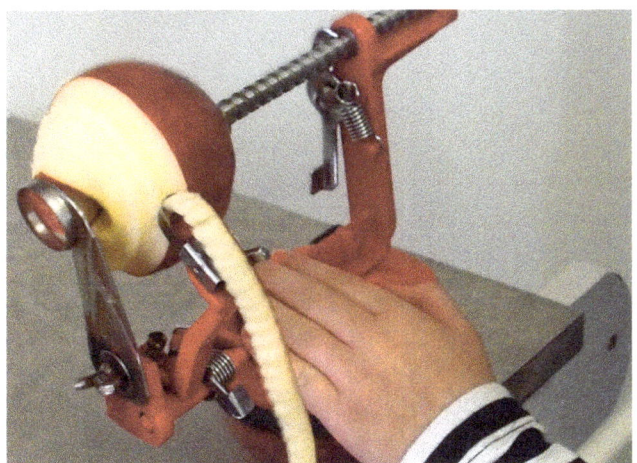

• A grater. This can be used for carrot, apple or cheese. Plus, there are beautiful fruit slicers available too.

• A masher for soft food such as cooked potatoes or eggs and raw food, such as avocado and bananas.

• A sifter. Try to access a rotary and a pump sifter for different hand actions.

• A garlic press can be used with garlic pieces, with play dough or a set of small sponges.

• Juicing apparatus, that is either mechanical or electric, are best used with seasonal fruits and vegetables.

• A grinder or mortar and pestle for such items as nutmeg, rock salt, coffee beans and eggshells.

• Dough cutters or bread punches for making biscuits or sandwiches. Provide a small knife for spreading.

• Play dough and tools such as squeezers and hammers. Add real kitchen tools such as pastry cutters, a rolling pin, knives and pots, as well as craft bits and items from nature.

• A mat with a depiction of where crockery and cutlery is positioned helps young children to manage the task of setting out table positions independently. These mats are common to Montessori stores.

• Different containers with lids, for example those that use skills such as screwing and pressing.

• Pegs used for pegging onto a line or plastic pots. These can include wooden dolly pegs, plastic household pegs or small craft pegs. Children can peg socks, cloths or felt pieces.

• A set of cloths or small clothes for folding.

• Scissors for cutting a variety of materials that suit the developmental level of the children, whether it is snipping, cutting on straight lines, cutting curves or cutting around an item on a page.

• Plastic tubing, ribbon or yarn for threading pasta, buttons, beads, leaves or paper or a darning needle with wool, for sewing card and material. A hole punch is useful for children to set up their threading materials such as paper and leaves and to punch card to sew.

• Real shoes or practice sets with real laces that assist with the learning of Velcro, buckles or laces.

• Socks or gloves to pair.

• A purse or wallet to practice zipping and clasps or a belt to work with buckles.

• A piggy bank with money or plastic buttons, used for posting.

• Locks and keys in different sizes.

• A little hammer and tacks with balsa wood or a corkboard, to suspend bits of wood. Alternatively, use golf tees with a foam box or dough.

• Tools such as a saw and glue gun for creating with wood.

• Nuts with bolts to practice twisting and grading skills.

• Some bees wax polish, a cloth or a brush for cleaning metal or wood.

- A set of screws and a screwdriver.

Chapter 5
FUNCTIONAL PLAY

In this chapter we explore functional play that stimulates both the sensory and motor pathways. It is termed functional play because it has the specific task of developing the physical and neurological pathways of the body to establish brain growth and build a solid foundation.

These activities are not wasteful on development, nor do they break family budgets or the environment, as many can be passed on or recycled. They are timeless and can be used over and over again. Many of these are based on items already found in the family home.

Here is a list of functional play activities for development:

- **STORE PURCHASED TOYS FOR MOTOR DEVELOPMENT**

These activities are often the 'toy' equivalent of the realistic work endeavours that children undertake. They are pertinent to some extent because they assist in building strength and coordination, as long as the children also practice real skills.

These toys should not form the basis of the environment, as real work is always best.

Ask:

What is the function in the particular toy or activity that adds to the skills of the children at a particular development level?

Are they reusable or recyclable?

Will they store well with order for the children?

Some examples of good functional motor toys for children include those for:

1. Hand Eye Coordination

2. Cutting skills

3. Locking

4. Hammering

5. Other Tool Skills

6. Construction Skills

7. Threading & Lacing

8. Twisting Skills
(similar to containers with lids)

- **STORE PURCHASED TOYS FOR SENSORY DEVELOPMENT**

There is a wonderful array of sensory activities available to children that really are a compliment to what is in the world. These beautifully designed apparatus stimulate vision, touch and auditory pathways to enhance learning.

The following is a selection of some of the best sensory apparatus available, however, in every store there is a much larger collection:

1. Size & shape awareness

2. Colour Awareness

3. Tracking with the Eye

4. Patterning & Sequencing with the Eye

5. Texture Awareness

6. Weight

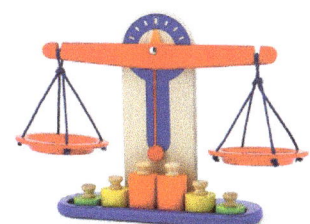

7. Sound Awareness

- **HOME MADE SENSORY AND MOTOR ACTIVITIES**

Home made sensory and motor activities are brilliant for development, the family budget, for the environment and for the relationship between adults and children.

"There is nothing better than developing a sensory and/or motor activity in an environment for young children, showing it to them, watching their faces and their discoveries, through sensing and manipulating it..."
and
"an adult needs to learn to collect, collect everyday for

materials that can instigate sensory and motor activity – from nature, from the supermarket and hardware store, from what comes in the post..." (Barker, 2014).

Here is a collection of materials and ideas for sensory and motor activities to make at home or childcare:

Water, sticks, bark, leaves, shells, shell grit, stones, feathers, seed pods, gum nuts, dirt, mud, snow, dried leaves, dried petals, ice, flour, corn flour, bi carbonate of soda, cream of tartar, vinegar, vegetable oil, food colouring, essences, polenta, icing sugar, coffee beans, egg shells, variety of pastas and beans, rice, oats, sunflower seeds, barley, buckwheat, lentils, rock salt, patty pans, straws, pots with lids that screw, pots without lids, funnels, a ladle, a masher, a tenderizer, a rolling pin, a garlic press, dough cutters, plastic knives, a muffin tin, metal trays, measuring cups, measuring spoons, a sieve or colander, beaters, sponges, baby shampoo and conditioner, isopropyl alcohol, shaving cream, Epsom salt, cotton wool or balls, cotton buds, foam pieces, packing foam, bubble wrap, cardboard pieces and rolls, old cards and calendars, magazines, cellophane, tinsel, lace, sandpaper of different grades, egg cartons, paper plates, paddle sticks, match sticks, glitter, pompoms, felt pieces, foam shapes, buttons, beads, plastic tubing, wool, ribbon, string, aquarium materials, fishing line, golf tees, pieces of balsa wood or thin wood, tacks, nuts and bolts, locks and keys, hooks and rings, washers, dowels, wood shavings.

A collection of realistic animals (farm, wild, ocean, bugs) and transport figures (land, sea and air) are a wonderful addition. Any of these should be realistic, for example, a lion should not be something from a cartoon or movie but a close depiction of what is seen in the wild.

Sensory troughs are amazing! They offer children both sensory and motor activity in one exercise. They also influence the attention and concentration span of children in a positive way. There are so many options from the materials above, that it's a matter of exploration! It's fun for adults as well as children!

Here are some examples, most of which are used with pots, ladles, funnels, measuring cups, measuring spoons or muffin tins. Animal and transport figures can be a welcome addition:

- A water play trough, with ladles and pots, shampoo for bubbles and sponges for squeezing; the water may be coloured with food dye.

• Coloured rice, pasta or navy beans with pots, spoons and a funnel (see Chapter 6).

• Oats, large or small beans, pasta, barley, buckwheat, bird seed or sunflower seeds.

• Polenta or rock salt with pots, funnels, paint brushes and ladles.

• A shaving cream trough.

• A goop or finger paint trough (see Chapter 6).

• A cloud or foam dough trough (see Chapter 6).

- Sand, mud or kinetic sand with spades, moulds and buckets.

- Rocks, pebbles, aquarium pebbles, shell grit in a tub - these can be used as a base for 'animal habitats' or to simply, fill and pour.

- Potpourri – rose petals are best.

- Water beads of single or mixed colours.

- Ice cubes or large ice cup moulds; these are wonderful coloured or with items frozen inside, use a small pick to remove the items as the ice melts.

• Gelatine moulds that are coloured or with items inside for the children to discover.

For a visual display of Sensory Trough ideas go to the Toddler Education Services Pty Ltd / Montessori 1:1 Blog, Instagram or Facebook pages:
www.toddlereducationservices.com.au/blog-articles
www.instagram.com/ruthbarker1970
www.facebook.com/Montessori11/photos_stream

Other ideas:

Vision:

• Use a light box to study colour and pattern. To build a light box go to:
www.toddlereducationservices.com.au/montessori-matters-5

- A series of discovery bottles – add for example, sand and distilled water, glitter and distilled water, oil and distilled water, dishwashing liquid in distilled water and items to sink and float.

- Mixing colours with pipettes and coloured water.

- A tray of bicarbonate of soda with coloured vinegar, use an eyedropper to drop the vinegar onto the bicarbonate of soda.

- A shallow dish of full fat milk with soapy coloured water to drop in with a dropper.

- Grading trays that are made with a set of similar items such as buttons, washers, bolts, nuts, nails, sockets, dowels, lids or anything else that increases in size.

- Grading trays for thickness.

Touch:

- Grading items that are light or heavy.

- Texture trays of hard and soft, rough and smooth or plastic/wood/glass/ceramic.

Sound:

• A series of sound jars from soft to loud - add for example, rice, beads, beans, rocks, water.

Smell:

• Making smell bottles with cotton wool and essences or oils.

• Making a smelling tray with foods.

For a visual display of these and other ideas go to the Toddler Education Services Pty Ltd / Montessori 1:1 Blog,

Instagram or Facebook pages:
www.toddlereducationservices.com.au/blog-articles
www.instagram.com/ruthbarker1970
www.facebook.com/Montessori11/photos_stream

The making of an **art centre** involves collecting the items from above and sorting these into an ordered display. The children can choose what they would like - these choices should be from nature as well as manmade. Put these together with scissors, a hole-punch, glue, tape, a stapler, string and/or ribbon. Keep a pile of paper, paper plates or brown paper bags for the children, who can then create when they feel they want to, rather than when they are told to.

The **outdoor environment** is a haven for sensory and motor activity. Children should be encouraged to spend every single day outdoors, no matter what the weather. This is because the weather is one of the most natural sensorial mediums for children.

It is best to let the children play!

Not much needs to be added to a natural environment for sensory and motor phenomena to occur! The more water, sand, mud, leaves, sticks, bark, rocks, rock pools and trees that little children can explore, the better for brain growth!

Add a water pit, a sand pit, a mud pit, a rock path, a swing, a slide, a cubby and a vehicle, shells or rocks, trucks and diggers, animal figures, buckets, funnels, pots, spades, water collecting containers, water wheels, colanders, sieves, piping, tubing, real tools such as hammers and hand drills with wood...

Let the children play! Let them explore! Let them create! And let them be... there is NO BETTER ACTIVITY FOR BODY AND BRAIN THAN BEING OUTDOORS.

Chapter 6

TEN RECIPES FOR SENSORY MOTOR FUN

1. Basic Play Dough

½ cup salt
1 cup plain flour
1 tbs oil
1 tsp cream of tartar
1 cup water with added colouring

Combine all of the ingredients into a saucepan and stir until it is a smooth paste. Add low heat and cook for around 5 min until a ball forms from stirring and lifting. Allow the dough to cool and knead it well. Store in an airtight container.

2. Cloud Dough and Foam Dough

1 cup of baby oil *or*
1 cup of conditioner (think of scent) *or*
1 cup of Sorbalene *or*
1 cup of shaving cream
mixed with
1 cup to 4 cups of corn flour *or*
1 cup to 6 cups of flour
(depending on wanted consistencies)

3. Finger Paint

½ cup corn flour
3 tbs sugar
½ tsp salt
2 cups water

Blend all ingredients together over low heat. Separate the portions into pots or jars (depending on the amount of colours) and add drops of food colour to each. Mix well.

4. Goop or Corn Flour Paint

2 cups corn flour
220 ml liquid starch (purchased online) *or*
220 ml warm water (not as effective)

Blend these together and separate into jars. Add desired colours.

5. Flubber and Slime

1 tsp Borax in 1 cup warm water *or*
1 cup of liquid starch (purchased online)
1 cup school PVA glue
food colours

Mix either ingredients with the school glue. Separate into pots and add desired food colours.

6. Instant Slime

1 cup Lux Flakes
2 litres warm water

Add Lux Flakes to warm water.

7. Homemade Paste

1 tbs plain flour
2 tbs corn flour
5 tbs of warm water

Mix the dry ingredients together in a saucepan, slowly add the water and continue to stir until the mixture becomes thick in consistency.

8. Bubbles

½ cup water
½ cup glycerine
1 tbs liquid detergent

Place the water into a container and add the other ingredients, stirring the mixture with a hand or rotary whisk. Pour onto an extra large sponge or use with a blowing implement.

9. Colouring Beans, Rice, Pasta or Sand

A zip lock bag for each colour
Isopropyl alcohol *or*
rubbing alcohol (available from a chemist)
food colours

Place the dry ingredient into as many bags as there are to be colours. Squirt in a Tlb spoon of isopropyl alcohol into each bag. Drop in the required colours. Zip lock very carefully and proceed to rub the ingredient around. Open the bag to air-dry the ingredient.

10. Ice Cube or Gelatine Moulds

Place either coloured water or gelatine in water into ice cube trays, moulds or in containers. Add some trinkets into the base - such as animal figures or shells. Freeze or cool.

NOTES

NOTES

Thank you for reading:

The Parenting 5

Sensory Motor Play for Little People

Also, available now:

The Parenting 5

Practical and Independent Little People

And, coming soon:

The Parenting 5

Developing Language and Literacy

The Mathematical Mind

The World Around Them

REFERENCES AND RECOMMENDATIONS

The books and academic study of Dr Maria Montessori (1870 - 1952).

The President and Fellows of Harvard College. In Brief Series (2013). Centre of the Developing Child.
www.developingchild.harvard.edu
- The Science of Early Childhood
- The Impact of Early Adversity on Brain Development
- Early Childhood Brain Effectiveness
- The Foundations of Life Long Health
- Early Childhood Mental Health

Barker,R. The Parenting 5 - Practical and Independent Little People (2013). Toddler Education Services Pty Ltd.
www.toddlereducationservices.com.au

Seven Up (1964). Granada Television.

Seldin,T. How to Raise an Amazing Child (2007). Dorling Kindersley.

Langford,J. Montessori Child. Blog (2014).
www.montessorichild.com.au

From Little Things
www.fromlittlethings.net.au

Cleverstuff
www.cleverstuff.com.au

Ruth Barker has developed these books for parents and carers to develop environments that assist children in reaching their potential. In doing so Ruth Barker has made all reasonable endeavours to ensure that the contents of these books are useful and accurate. There is no duty of care between Ruth Barker and the readers.

Under no circumstances will Ruth Barker be liable for any loss or damage, including but not limited to, direct, indirect or consequential losses, including any form of consequential loss such as third party loss, loss of profits, loss of revenue, loss of opportunity, pure economic loss and an increased operating cost, personal injury or death however sustained in connection with:
• The Reader's reliance on these books
• Any inaccurate or incorrect information presented by Ruth Barker or,
• Any act or omission (whether negligent or not) of Ruth Barker.

Readers release and discharge and at all times will indemnify and keep indemnified Ruth Barker against any loss (including reasonable legal costs and expenses) claims, liabilities or expenses of any kinds, incurred or in connection with:
• Adverse consequences due to the Readers reliance on the materials in these books
• Any act or omission (whether negligent or not) of the Reader to any third parties/or
• Any damage, harm or violence caused by the Reader to any third parties.

www.ingramcontent.com/pod-product-compliance
Lightning Source LLC
LaVergne TN
LVHW010317070426
835507LV00026B/3435